Lovely Tatting

DOILIES *for* SPRING *and* SUMMER

HYE-OON LEE

Contents

Introduction

I came across tatting twenty-five years ago at a local craft store. As a stay-at-home mom raising two daughters, I wanted to fill my home with decorations made with my own two hands. The first craft I picked up was cross-stitch. One by one, I finished a number of designs to decorate the walls. Soon afterwards, I moved on to needlepoint, punch needle, and embroidery as well.

Having decorated the walls, I then grew interested in adding embellishment to table surfaces. I went to my favorite local craft store to find some crochet doily patterns. As I was browsing the aisles, a very delicate doily on display caught my eye. It looked different from crochet doilies. That was when I discovered tatting. I immediately signed up for a tatting class that day, and purchased my first tatting shuttles.

In tatting class, we began by learning how to wind thread onto a shuttle. Then, our instructor showed us how to make the basic tatting knot, the double stitch. She made it look so effortless in her demonstration that I thought it would be easy, but it took me a couple tries to get it right. I was motivated by the challenge of learning something new and creating something delicate and beautiful.

For the first couple of months, I was happy following existing patterns in books. But after a while, I began to imagine my own designs. I wanted to express my own point of view and create new patterns with a more modern look. Ideas would pop up in my head, even while I was asleep. I designed several dozen patterns in those years.

When my daughters were in grade school, I started to work in real estate in order to provide some extra support. During those years, I put aside my tatting shuttles.

I started tatting again in 2010, during the global economic recession when the real estate business was severely impacted. My family suggested that I start tatting again, knowing that I was passionate about creating new patterns.

I took out the box where I had stored all of my old tatting supplies and tried to pick up where I had left off. But even though I had a lot of experience tatting, it had been many years since I picked up my shuttles and it took me a while to jog my muscle memory. When I did a quick search on the Internet to remember some techniques, I learned that many new techniques were in use. Excited to learn these new techniques, I sought out a local instructor named Sabina Madden, who provided very thorough insight and knowledge.

We met for two hours, once a week, for three months. Knowing that I was used to tatting the old way, Sabina challenged me to cast aside my fixed knowledge of tatting. One of the first lessons she taught me was that the traditional way of making a knot did not differentiate the right side from the wrong side. She also taught me that there was no need to reverse the work when making chains. Traditionally, people would reverse the work when making chains after rings and vice versa. Sabina showed me the 'wrapping double stitch,' which allows the tatter to make chains entirely on the right side of the work.

Many of the patterns in this book utilize these new techniques and I am deeply grateful to Sabina for teaching them to me.

What began as an effort to fill my home with handmade decorations has turned into a lifelong passion for tatting. I would not have been able to do it without the constant support from my family. I am especially grateful for my daughter, Eunice, for all the work that she contributed to this book. She designed these pages, took all the photos, and helped me with editing despite having a busy schedule. Without her help, this book would not have come to life. I hope that my patterns inspire more people to pick up this elegant art.

Hye-oon Lee

What Is Tatting?

Tatting is a lace-making technique that consists of creating a series of knots. The knots become rings and/or chains which can then be joined to create the lace object. Until a ring is closed or a chain is finished, the knots can be moved along the thread, with the thread being the axis of movement. Therefore, the tatting knot can be called a 'moving knot.' Tatting can be used to create a number of embellishments, including doilies, collars, edgings for handkerchiefs or tables, ornaments, frames, and jewelry.

Tatting has evolved over the years, with new techniques enhancing or replacing existing ones. Two of these newer techniques include the 'front and back side technique' and the 'continuous method.' Traditionally, there was no differentiation between the right side and the wrong side of work. With the new front and back side technique, all full double stitches are on the right side of the work. Another important development in tatting is the continuous method, which uses the techniques 'split ring' and 'split chain.' Split ring and split chain make it possible to move to the next row or round without cutting the thread. These techniques will be used throughout this book.

Shuttle Tatting

In shuttle tatting, the shuttle is the main tool used to create tatted lace. Other ways to tat include needle tatting and cro-tatting. However, this book will focus on shuttle tatting. A typical shuttle is about three inches long and about half an inch wide. Shuttles are usually made of plastic, but can also be made of other materials such as metal, shell, and bone. Some shuttles have a bobbin and others have a hole in the center.

Materials

Shuttles

It is good to have several shuttles on hand, since some patterns require multiple shuttles.

Thread

The higher the number, the finer the thread.

Crochet hooks

Crochet hooks are used to join elements and incorporate beads into the work. For the thread specified in this book, use crochet hooks between 0.60mm and 1.00mm.

Scissors

Scissors are necessary to snip the remaining thread tails.

Needle threader

A needle threader is used to easily thread a sewing needle.

Sewing needles

Sewing needles are used to hide the remaining thread tails into adjacent stitches.

Picot gauge

A picot gauge is used to measure picots, ensuring that they are even in length.

Tacky glue

Tacky glue can be an alternative to using sewing needles to hide the remaining thread tails. A toothpick can come in handy when applying the glue.

Techniques

WINDING THREAD

Single shuttle

Pull the thread through the hole of the bobbin and tie it (figure 1). Pull the shuttle to tighten the knot close to the bobbin. Then, start winding thread onto the shuttle.

figure 1

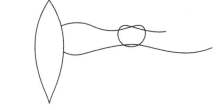

Continuous thread method

Pull the thread through the hole of the bobbin and tie it. Pull the shuttle to tighten the knot close to the bobbin. Then, start winding thread onto the shuttle. Use the ball of thread as a second 'shuttle' (figure 2). Alternatively, the ball of thread can be winded onto a second shuttle (figure 3).

figure 2

figure 3

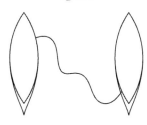

Weaver's knot

A weaver's knot is used to tie together two separate threads (figure 4).

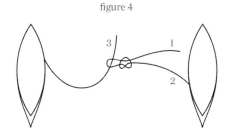

figure 4

After positioning the two threads as in the illustration above, pull thread 1 and thread 2 at the same time, forming a knot around thread 3. There should be a small popping sound.

MAKING A KNOT

(Flipping) double stitch

The double stitch is the basis of tatting.

Let approximately 12 inches of the shuttle thread hang loose from the back of the shuttle. Hold the shuttle in the right hand and the free end of the shuttle thread between the thumb and forefinger of the left hand. Bring the thread around the fingers of the left hand to form a circle and cross the thread under the thumb (figure 5).

figure 5: hand position when making a ring

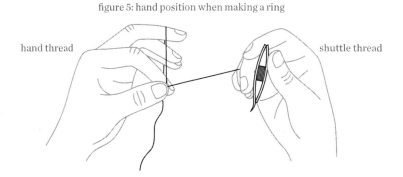

hand thread

shuttle thread

First half stitch: Forming a loop between the first and second fingers over the back of the left hand, bring the shuttle thread to the front over the hand thread. Then put the shuttle thread under the hand thread, pull it through the formed loop, and flip the hand thread over the straight shuttle thread as an axis to make the stitch (figures 6a, 6b, and 6c).

figure 6a

figure 6b

figure 6c

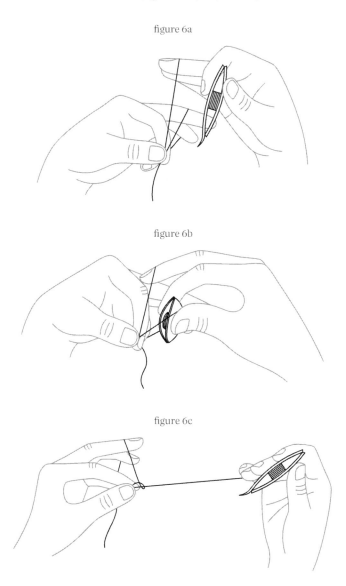

Second half stitch: Forming a loop at the front side of the hand thread, bring the shuttle thread to the back over the hand thread, put the shuttle thread under the hand thread, and pull it up through the formed loop. Then flip the hand thread over the straight shuttle thread as an axis to make the stitch (figures 7a, 7b, and 7c).

figure 7a

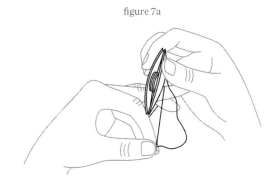

figure 7b

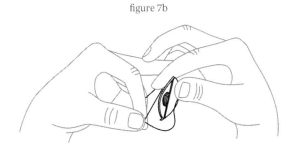

figure 7c

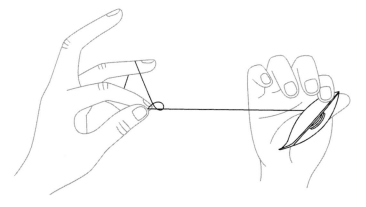

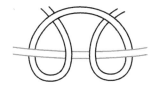

Hand position when making a chain

To make a chain on the wrong side, reverse the work vertically after a ring is made. Wind the hand thread onto the fifth finger (refer to figure 9 for the left hand position). Start with the second half stitch, then follow with the first half stitch of the flipping double stitch so that the full double stitch is on the right side.

Wrapping double stitch

The wrapping double stitch allows both rings and chains to be made entirely on the right side of the work. There is no need to reverse the work. Chains made with this technique are called 'direct method chains.' The wrapping double stitch is used especially for the second part of split rings. The shuttle thread is wrapped over the hand thread as the axis.

First half stitch: Proceed with the second half stitch of the flipping double stitch, wrapping the shuttle thread over the hand thread (figure 9).

Second half stitch: Proceed with the first half stitch of the flipping double stitch, wrapping the shuttle thread over the hand thread.

figure 9

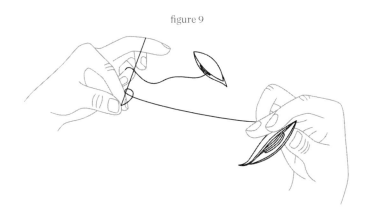

MAKING A PICOT

A picot is simply a loop, created by leaving extra thread space between stitches.

JOINING ELEMENTS

Picot Join

Down join: When joining happens on the right side of the work, put the hand thread over the picot. Using a crochet hook, pull the hand thread down through the picot, and make a loop without twisting it. Bring the shuttle thread into the loop in the direction of front to back (figure 10), expand the hand thread, and then adjust the tension. It becomes the first half stitch of the knot. Finish the knot with the second half stitch.

Up join: When joining happens on the wrong side of the work, put the hand thread under the picot. Using a crochet hook, pull the hand thread up through the picot, and make a loop without twisting it. Bring the shuttle thread into the loop in the direction of front to back (figure 10), expand the hand thread, and then adjust the tension. It becomes the second half stitch of the knot. Finish the knot with the first half stitch.

figure 10

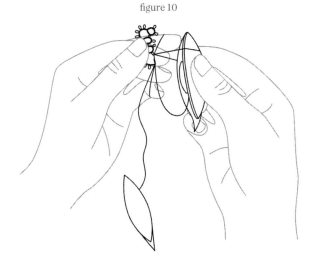

Shuttle Lock Join (SLJ)

A shuttle lock join is used to finish work.

Down join: A down join happens on the right side of the work. Using a crochet hook, pull the shuttle thread down through the finished ring or chain, and make a loop without twisting it. Bring the shuttle thread into the loop in the direction of front to back, adjust the tension, and tighten the ends.

Up join: An up join happens on the wrong side of the work. Using a crochet hook, pull the shuttle thread up through the finished ring or chain, and make a loop without twisting it. Bring the shuttle thread into the loop in the direction of back to front, adjust the tension, and tighten the ends.

Split Ring Join (SRJ)

A split ring join is used to join the second part of a split ring. When the join is on the right side, put Sh2 over the work and do the up picot join. Adjust the hand thread so that the first stitch works as a wrapping stitch. Then follow with the second half wrapping stitch. When the join is on the wrong side, put Sh2 under the work and do the down picot join. Adjust the hand thread so that the first stitch works as a wrapping stitch. Then follow with the first half wrapping stitch.

HANDLING REMAINING THREAD TAILS

Remaining thread tails at the beginning of work

One thread tail: Put the tail into the loop formed when making a ring so that it is parallel with the shuttle thread. Repeat it for about three times, close the ring, and then snip the remaining tail.

Two thread tails: When two separate threads were tied using the weaver's knot, hide the thread tail of the shuttle when making a ring in the same way as in the case for one thread tail. Hide the second thread tail when making a chain so that it is parallel with the hand thread. The remaining steps will be the same as in the case for one thread tail.

Remaining thread tails in the middle of work

Cut the remaining tail of either a shuttle or hand thread to about 2 inches in length and put it together with the tail of newly winded thread into the formed loop when making knots. The remaining steps will be the same as for the beginning of work.

Remaining thread tails at the end of work

Thread the tail through a sewing needle and sew it into the adjacent stitches three or four times to hide the thread, and then snip it with a scissor. Alternatively, cut the tail and attach the ends to the work using a tiny dab of tacky glue.

Abbreviations & Notations

Sh1 Shuttle one

Sh2 Shuttle two

— A decorative or connecting picot, its height is about the length of three double stitches.

—— A decorative or connecting picot, its height is double the length of —.

——— A decorative or connecting picot, its height is triple the length of —, or approximately 5/16 inch.

———— A decorative or connecting picot, its height is quadruple the length of —, or approximately 3/8 inch or 1/2 inch.

- A construction or connecting picot, its height is the length of one double stitch.

-- A construction or connecting picot, its height is double the length of -.

—- A decorative or connecting picot, its height is the sum of the lengths of — & -.

—-- A decorative or connecting picot, its height is the sum of the lengths of — & --.

+ An indication to join elements through a picot or the base of a ring. It is used for the picot join, SLJ, and SRJ.

^ When making a split ring (SR), it denotes the stitches of Sh1 and Sh2. For example, SR 5^5 indicates five double stitches with Sh1 and five double stitches with Sh2.

X An indication of the number of picots in a ring or a chain. For example, R 5 X 4 means to repeat four times the making of five double stitches followed by a picot. It is the same as R 5—5—5—5.

d First half stitch

s Second half stitch

5d/5s An indication to make five first half stitches followed by five second half stitches.

5s/5d An indication to make five second half stitches followed by five first half stitches.

* * An indication to repeat the content between * and *. It is also an indication to repeat the content between * and * to the end of the round.

*** *** An indication to repeat the content between *** and *** to the end of the round. It is used when * and * is also used in the same round to differentiate the two.

<> An indication to copy the instructions between < and >. In a single round, the first instance of < and > will show instructions between them. The second instance will only show <>.

{} Denotes a clover leaf consisting of adjacent rings.

R Ring

Ch Chain

p Picot

RW Reverse work is an indication to turn over the work vertically. It occurs when making a chain after a ring and when making a ring after a chain in the traditional way. Since making a chain is possible on the right side with the wrapping double stitch, RW has not been used in most of the patterns, with the exception of a few of the patterns in order to indicate direction.

JR A Josephine ring is a ring made with the first half stitches on the right side and with the second half stitches on the wrong side.

JK A Josephine knot is a chain made with the first half stitches on the right side and with the second half stitches on the wrong side.

SLJ If the next round starts with SR after SLJ, continue the work. Otherwise, SLJ implies finishing the work by hiding the ends.

Hide Ends Cut thread and use a needle to sew it into adjacent stitches. Then, use a small dab of tacky glue to secure thread to work.

SR A split ring is used to start a new round that continues from the previous round.

Tat the first half of a ring with Sh1 and drop Sh1. Hand Sh1 over the back of the left hand. Turn the hand thread counter-clockwise. Pinch the area of the first double stitch. With Sh2, tat the desired number of wrapping double stitches (refer to figure 9). Close the split ring with Sh1.

SCh A split chain is used on the last chain in a round of a work. It is a new technique that makes it possible to move from one round to another without cutting thread. After making the desired number of knots of a chain in the usual way, make the remaining number of knots of the same chain backwards with the shuttle. Do the up-SLJ to the base of the first ring of the round, leaving thread space to make the remaining knots. Pull the shuttle from front to back, making a loop, and send the shuttle from front to back. It becomes the first half stitch. Leave the loop loose. Pull the shuttle from back to front to make the loop again and send the shuttle from back to front. It becomes the second half stitch. Tighten the thread tension of the first and second half stitches.

If a split chain happens to be on the right side, do the down-SLJ along with the steps involved in reverse order.

MR A mock ring is a chain that resembles a ring. To make a mock ring, form a loop about 2 inches long with the shuttle thread downward. Pinch the end point with the thumb and index finger of the left hand and start a new chain. Then pull the shuttle through the formed loop from back to front. Tighten the chain to form a mock ring.

MP A mock picot is used in the following two cases:

First Case: Where a regular picot cannot be made either at the base of a ring or the inside of a chain, make thread space with a paper clip before starting a ring or a chain.

Second Case: When making a ring with a specified number of picots, make the last picot using the lock stitch technique. Using a single shuttle, leave 6 inches of thread space when starting a ring. Use the thread space as the shuttle thread. Using two shuttles, use Sh2 as the shuttle thread. This technique makes it possible to move on to the next step without cutting thread.

Example: If a ring has six picots, make five picots and close the ring. Make the sixth picot (mock picot) using the lock stitch technique with the thread space or Sh2 as the shuttle thread.

SLT The shoe lace trick is a simple technique to exchange the positions of the shuttle thread and the hand thread, and resembles the movement of tying a shoe lace. The hand thread becomes the shuttle thread and vice versa. It is necessary when making a direct chain without reversing the work or when matching colors when two different colors are being used.

Lock Stitch A lock stitch is a technique to prevent knots from moving, and is used when making a mock picot. To make a lock stitch, start with the second half of a wrapping stitch followed by the second half of a flipping stitch.

How to Read Patterns

Example 1

R 4—3—3—4, Ch 4—6—4. *R 4+3—3—4, Ch 4—6—4.* Repeat * * 6 more times.

Explanation: The R 4+3—3—4 portion of the above example implies joining to the last p of the last ring. In the last ring, the last picot indicates joining the last ring to the first p of the first ring, closing the round.

Example 2

SR 6ˆ6, Ch 4-4. *[R 6+6 (to next Ch p on previous round)], Ch 4-4.*

Explanation: Work SR 6ˆ6 and Ch 4-4. Then repeat the steps within the asterisks.

Example 3

SR 3ˆ3, <Ch 4, R 10+10 (to base of next R on previous round), Ch 4, *R 3+3, Ch 3-3,* repeat * * 2 more times>. ***R 3+3, <>.*** SCh at last 3 ds.

Explanation: Work SR 3ˆ3 and the steps within the <>. Continue to work R 3+3. The following empty <> indicates to work the steps within the previous <>. Continue to work SCh at last 3 ds.

Example 4

Ch 2-2+ (to next Ch p on previous round).

Explanation: Work Ch 2-2 and do the SLJ to the next Ch p on previous round.

Cherry Blossom Motif 1

MATERIALS

2 tatting shuttles

DMC Cordonnet, size 30

SIZE

3 inches

INSTRUCTIONS

Round 1: R 7-3-3-7, leave 1/8 inch of thread. *R 7+3-3-7, leave 1/8 inch of thread.* Repeat * * 13 more times. Last R as SR 7+3ˆ7+3 (SRJ to first p of first R). Total 16 Rs.

Round 2: SR 6ˆ6, Ch 8 [Sh2: {R 6-4-2, R 2+3—3—3—3-2, R 2+4-6}] 8. *R 6+6 (to next R p on previous round), Ch 8 [Sh2: {R 6+4-2, R 2+3—3—3—3-2, R 2+4-6}] 8.* SLJ.

Cherry Blossom Motif 2

MATERIALS

2 tatting shuttles

DMC Cordonnet, size 30

SIZE

3.5 inches

INSTRUCTIONS

Round 1: R 7-3-3-7, leave 1/8 inch of thread. *R 7+ 3-3-7, leave 1/8 inch of thread.* Repeat * * 13 more times. Last R as SR 7+3ˆ7+3 (SRJ to first p of first R). Total 16 Rs.

Round 2: SR 6ˆ6, Ch 8 [Sh2: {R 6-4-2, R 2+3—3—3—3-2, R 2+4-6}] 8. *R 6+6 (to next R p on previous round), Ch 8 [Sh2: {R 6+4-2, R 2+3—3—3—3-2, R 2+4-6}] 8.* SLJ.

Round 3: R 7-3+ (to any middle R p on previous round) 3-7, Ch 3—3, *R 7+ 3—3-7, Ch 3—3,* repeat * * 1 more time. ***R 7+3+3-7, Ch 3—3, *R 7+3—3-7, Ch 3—3,* repeat * * 1 more time.*** SLJ.

Cherry Blossom Motif 3

MATERIALS

2 tatting shuttles

DMC Cordonnet, size 30

SIZE

4.25 inches

INSTRUCTIONS

Round 1: R 7-3-3-7, leave 1/8 inch of thread. *R 7+3-3-7, leave 1/8 inch of thread.* Repeat * * 13 more times. Last R as SR 7+3ˆ7+3 (SRJ to first p of first R). Total 16 Rs.

Round 2: SR 6ˆ6, Ch 8 [Sh2: {R 6-4-2, R 2+3—3—3—3-2, R 2+4-6}] 8. *R 6+6 (to next R p on previous round), Ch 8 [Sh2: {R 6+4-2, R 2+3—3—3—3-2, R 2+4-6}] 8.* SLJ.

Round 3: *R 3—3+3—3 (to any middle R p on previous round), Ch 10-2 [Sh2: {R 2+ (to last Ch p) 4—4-2, R 2+3—3—3—3-2, R 2+4—4-2}] 2+ (to last p of last R) 10.* SLJ.

Cherry Blossom Doily 1

MATERIALS

2 tatting shuttles

DMC Cordonnet, size 30

SIZE

5 inches

INSTRUCTIONS

Round 1: R 7-3-3-7, leave 1/8 inch of thread. *R 7+3-3-7, leave 1/8 inch of thread.* Repeat * * 13 more times. Last R as SR 7+3ˆ7+3 (SRJ to first p of first R). Total 16 Rs.

Round 2: SR 6ˆ6, Ch 8 [Sh2: {R 6-4-2, R 2+3—3—3—3-2, R 2+4-6}] 8. *R 6+6 (to next R p on previous round), Ch 8 [Sh2: {R 6+4-2, R 2+3—3—3—3-2, R 2+4-6}] 8.* SLJ.

Round 3: R 3—3+ (to any middle R p on previous round) 3—3, Ch 12 [MR 3 (R 7—3—3-7) 2 (R 7+3—3-7) 2 (R 7+3—3-7) 2 (R 7+3—3-7) 2 (R 7+3—3—7) 3] 12. *R 3—3+3—3, Ch 12 [MR 3 (R 7+3—3-7) 2 (R 7+3—3-7) 2 (R 7+3—3-7) 2 (R 7+3—3-7) 2 (R 7+3—3—7) 3] 12.* SLJ.

Cherry Blossom Doily 2

MATERIALS

2 tatting shuttles

DMC Cordonnet, size 30

SIZE

7.5 inches

INSTRUCTIONS

Round 1: R 7-3-3-7, leave 1/8 inch of thread. *R 7+3-3-7, leave 1/8 inch of thread.* Repeat * * 13 more times. Last R as SR 7+3ˆ7+3 (SRJ to first p of first R). Total 16 Rs.

Round 2: SR 6ˆ6, Ch 8 [Sh2: {R 6-4-2, R 2+3—3—3—3-2, R 2+4-6}] 8. *R 6+6 (to next R p on previous round, Ch 8 [Sh2: {R 6-4-2, R 2+3—3—3—3-2, R 2+4-6}] 8.* SLJ.

Round 3: R 7-3+ (to any middle R p on previous round) 3-7, Ch 3-3, *R 7+3—3-7, Ch 3-3,* repeat * * 1 more time. ***R 7+3+3-7, Ch 3-3, *R 7+3—3-7, Ch 3-3,* repeat * * 1 more time.*** SCh at last 3 ds.

Round 4: SR 6ˆ6, Ch 4-4. *R 6+6 (to next Ch p on previous round), Ch 4-4.* SCh at last 4 ds.

Round 5: SR 6ˆ6, Ch 5-5. *R 6+6 (to next Ch p on previous round), Ch 5-5.* SCh at 5 last ds.

Round 6: SR 6ˆ6, Ch 6-6. *R 6+6 (to next Ch p on previous round), Ch 6-6.* SCh at 6 ds.

Round 7: SR 6ˆ6, Ch 7-7. *R 6+6 (to next Ch p on previous round), Ch 7-7.* SCh at 7 ds.

Round 8: SR 6ˆ6, Ch 8 [Sh2: {R 6-4-2, R 2+3—3—3—3—3-2, R 2+4-6}] 8. *R 6+6 (to next Ch p on previous round), Ch 8 [Sh2: {R 6-4-2, R 2+3—3—3—3—3-2, R 2+4-6}] 8.* SLJ.

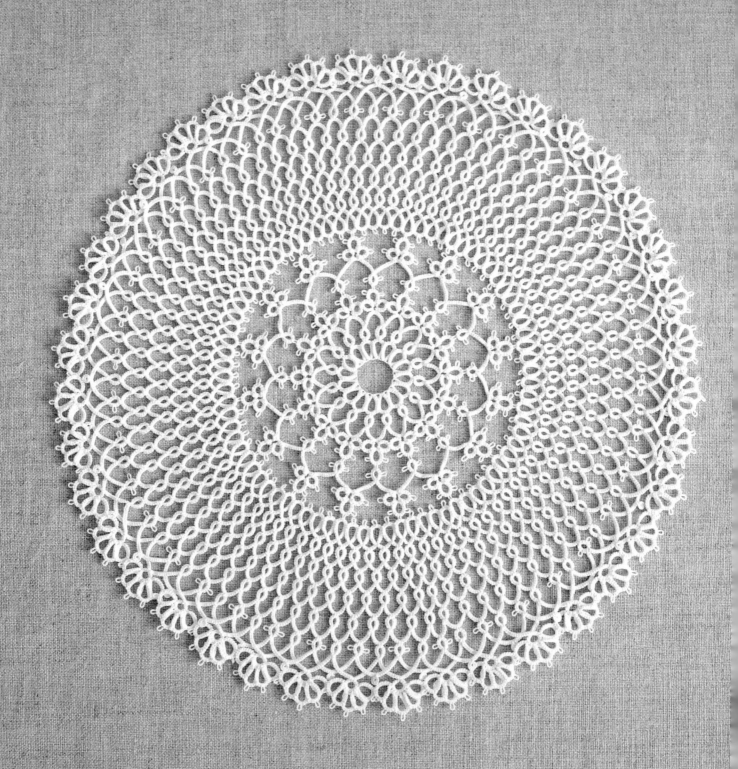

Cherry Blossom Doily 3

MATERIALS

2 tatting shuttles

DMC Cordonnet, size 30

SIZE

10 inches

INSTRUCTIONS

Round 1: R 7-3-3-7, leave 1/8 inch of thread. *R 7+3-3-7, leave 1/8 inch of thread.* Repeat * * 13 more times. Last R as SR 7+3ˆ7+3 (SRJ to first p of first R). Total 16 Rs.

Round 2: SR 6ˆ6, Ch 8 [Sh2: {R 6-4-2, R 2+3—3—3—3-2, R 2+4-6}] 8. *R 6+6 (to next R p on previous round), Ch 8 [Sh2: {R 6+4-2, R 2+3—3—3—3-2, R 2+4-6}] 8.* SLJ.

Round 3: *R 3—3+3—3 (to any middle R p on previous round), Ch 10-2 [Sh2: {R 2+ (to last Ch p) 4—4-2, R 2+3—3—3—3-2, R 2+4—4-2}] 2+ (to last p of last R) 10.* SLJ.

Round 4: R 7-3+ (to any middle R p on previous round) 3-7, Ch 3-3, *R 7+ 3—3-7, Ch 3-3,* repeat * * 3 more times. ***R 7+3+3-7, Ch 3-3, *R 7+3—3-7, Ch 3-3,* repeat * *3 more times.*** SCh at last 3 ds.

Round 5: SR 6ˆ6, Ch 4-4. *R 6+6 (to next Ch p on previous round), Ch 4-4.* SCh at last 4 ds.

Round 6: SR 6ˆ6, Ch 5-5. *R 6+6 (to next Ch p on previous round), Ch 5-5.* SCh at last 5 ds.

Round 7: SR 6ˆ6, Ch 6-6. *R 6+6 (to next Ch p on previous round), Ch 6-6.* SCh at last 6 ds.

Round 8: SR 6ˆ6, Ch 7-7. *R 6+6 (to next Ch p on previous round), Ch 7-7.* SCh at last 7 ds.

Round 9a: SR 6ˆ6, Ch 14 [MR 3 (R 7-3—3-7) 2 (R 7+3—3-7) 2 (R 7+3—3-7) 2 (R 7+3—3-7) 2 (R 7+3—3-7) 3] 14. *R 6+6 (to next middle R p on previous round, skipping one), Ch 14 [MR 3 (R 7-3—3-7) 2 (R 7+3—3-7) 2 (R 7+3—3-7) 2 (R 7+3—3-7) 2 (R 7+3—3-7) 3] 14.* SLJ.

Round 9b: *R 3—3+ (to any skipped middle R p on previous round) 3—3, Ch 14 [Sh2: JR 12] 14.* SLJ.

Frances Doily

MATERIALS

2 tatting shuttles (Sh1: white thread, Sh2: pink thread)

DMC Cebelia, size 30

SIZE

7.75 inches

INSTRUCTIONS

Round 1: R 1 X 18 (——— or 3/8 inch p), close R, make last p with Lock Stitch with Sh2. Total 18 ps.

Round 2: *Ch 2-2 + (to next p on previous round).* SCh at last 2 ds.

Round 3: SR 4ˆ4, Ch 6. *R 4+4 (to next Ch p on previous round), Ch 6.* SLJ.

Round 4: SR 4ˆ4, Ch 4 [Sh2: JR 7] 4. *R 4+4 (to base of next R on previous round), Ch 4 [Sh2: JR 7] 4.* SLJ.

Round 5: SR 4ˆ4, Ch 10. *R 4+4 (to base of next R on previous round), Ch 10.* SLJ.

Round 6: SR 4ˆ4, Ch 6 [Sh2: JR 7] 6. *R 4+4 (to base of next R on previous round), Ch 6 [Sh2: JR 7] 6.* SLJ.

Round 7: SR 4ˆ4, Ch 14. *R 4+4 (to base of next R on previous round), Ch 14.* SLJ.

Round 8: SR 4ˆ4, Ch 8 [Sh2: JR 7] 8. *R 4+4 (to base of next R on previous round), Ch 8 [Sh2: JR 7] 8.* SLJ.

Round 9: SR 4ˆ4, Ch 18. *R 4+4 (to base of next R on previous round), Ch 18.* SLJ.

Round 10: SR 4ˆ4, Ch 10 [Sh2: JR 7] 10. *R 4+4 (to base of next R on previous round), Ch 10 [Sh2: JR 7] 10.* SLJ.

Round 11: SR 4ˆ4, Ch 22. *R 4+4 (to base of next R on previous round), Ch 22.* SLJ.

Round 12: SR 4ˆ4, Ch 12 [Sh2: JR 7] 12. *R 4+4 (to base of next R on previous round), Ch 12 [Sh2: JR 7] 12.* SLJ.

Round 13: SR 4—4ˆ4—4, Ch 6-6-6-6-6. *R 4—4+4—4 (to base of next R on previous round), Ch

6-6-6-6-6.* SCh at last 6 ds.

Round 14: SR 3ˆ3, <Ch 4, R 10+10 (to base of next R on previous round), Ch 4, *R 3+3, Ch 3-3,* repeat * * 2 more times>. ***R 3+3, <>.*** SCh at last 3 ds.

Round 15: SR 3ˆ3, <Ch 4, R 11+11 (to base of next R on previous round), Ch 9, R 11+11 (to same R base), Ch 4, *R 3+3, Ch 3-3,* repeat * * 1 more time>. ***R 3+3, <>.*** SCh at last 3 ds.

Round 16: SR 3ˆ3, <Ch 4, R 11+11 (to base of next R on previous round), Ch 12, R 12+12 (over Ch between 2 Rs), Ch 12, R 11+11, Ch 4, R 3+3, Ch 3-3>. *R 3+3, <>.* SCh at last 3 ds.

Round 17: SR 3ˆ3, <Ch 4, R 11+11 (to base of next R on previous round), Ch 12, R 12+12 (over Ch between 2 Rs), Ch 12, R 12+12, Ch 12, R 12+12 (over Ch), Ch 12, R 11+11, Ch 4>. *R 3+3, <>.* SLJ.

Note: The doily in these photos was tatted without the SR technique. When tatted with the SR technique, as in the instructions, each SR will show two colors.

Ranunculus Doily 1

MATERIALS

2 tatting shuttles

DMC Cebelia, size 30

SIZE

9.5 inches

INSTRUCTIONS

Round 1: R 1 X 24 (——— or 3/8 inch p), close R, make last p with Lock Stitch with Sh2. Total 24 ps.

Round 2: *Ch 1-1+ (to next p on previous round).* SCh at last 1 ds.

Round 3: SR 2ˆ2, Ch 2-2. *R 2+2 (to next Ch p on previous round), Ch 2-2.* SCh at last 2 ds.

Round 4: SR 2ˆ2, Ch 3-3. *R 2+2 (to next Ch p on previous round), Ch 3-3.* SCh at last 3 ds.

Round 5: SR 2ˆ2, Ch 4-4. *R 2+2 (to next Ch p on previous round), Ch 4-4.* SCh at last 4 ds.

Round 6: SR 2ˆ2, Ch 5-5. *R 2+2 (to next Ch p on previous round), Ch 5-5.* SCh at last 5 ds.

Round 7: SR 2ˆ2, Ch 6-6. *R 2+2 (to next Ch p on previous round), Ch 6-6.* SCh at last 6 ds.

Round 8: SR 2ˆ2, Ch 8-8. *R 2+2 (to next Ch p on previous round), Ch 8-8.* SCh at last 8 ds.

Round 9: SR 2ˆ2, Ch 10-10. *R 2+2 (to next Ch p on previous round), Ch 10-10.* SCh at last 10 ds.

Round 10: SR 2ˆ2, Ch 12-12. *R 2+2 (to next Ch p on previous round), Ch 12-12.* SCh at last 12 ds.

Round 11: SR 3—3ˆ3—3, Ch 11-11. *R 3—3+3—3 (to next Ch p on previous round), Ch 11-11.* SCh at last 11 ds.

Round 12: SR 2ˆ2, <Ch 12, R 6+6 (to base of next R on previous round), Ch 12>. *R 2+2, <>.* SLJ.

Round 13: SR 6ˆ6, <Ch 13, R 6+6 (to base of next R on previous round), Ch 13>. *R 6+6, <>.* SLJ.

Round 14: SR 6ˆ6, <Ch 14, R 3—3+3—3 (to base of next R on previous round), Ch 14>. *R 6+6, <>.* SLJ.

Round 15: SR 6ˆ6, <Ch 15, R 6+6 (to base of next R on previous round), Ch 15>. *R 6+6, <>.* SLJ.

Round 16: SR 6ˆ6, <Ch 16, R 6+6 (to base of next R on previous round), Ch 16>. *R 6+6, <>.* SLJ.

Round 17: SR 6ˆ6, <Ch 17, R 3—3+3—3 (to base of next R on previous round), Ch 17>. *R 6+6, <>.* SLJ.

Round 18: SR 6ˆ6, <Ch 18, R 6+6 (to base of next R on previous round), Ch 18>. *R 6+6, <>.* SLJ.

Round 19: SR 6ˆ6, <Ch 19, R 6+6 (to base of next R on previous round), Ch 19>. *R 6+6, <>.* SLJ.

Round 20: SR 3—3ˆ3—3, Ch 5 [Sh2: JR 10] 5 [Sh2: JR 10] 5 [Sh2: JR 10] 5. *R 3—3+ (to base of next R on previous round) 3—3, Ch 5 [Sh2: JR 10] 5 [Sh2: JR 10] 5 [Sh2: JR 10] 5.* SLJ.

Ranunculus Doily 2

MATERIALS

2 tatting shuttles (Sh1: pink thread, Sh2: purple thread)

DMC Cebelia, size 30

SIZE

12 inches

INSTRUCTIONS

Round 1: R 1 X 24 (——— or 3/8 inch p), close R, make last p with Lock Stitch with Sh2. Total 24 ps.

Round 2: *Ch 1-1+ (to next p on previous round).* SCh at last 1 ds.

Round 3: SR 2^2, Ch 2-2. *R 2+2 (to next Ch p on previous round), Ch 2-2.* SCh at last 2 ds.

Round 4: SR 2^2, Ch 3-3. *R 2+2 (to next Ch p on previous round), Ch 3-3.* SCh at last 3 ds.

Round 5: SR 2^2, Ch 4-4. *R 2+2 (to next Ch p on previous round), Ch 4-4.* SCh at last 4 ds.

Round 6: SR 2^2, Ch 5-5. *R 2+2 (to next Ch p on previous round), Ch 5-5.* SCh at last 5 ds.

Round 7: SR 2^2, Ch 6-6. *R 2+2 (to next Ch p on previous round), Ch 6-6.* SCh at last 6 ds.

Round 8: SR 2^2, Ch 8-8. *R 2+2 (to next Ch p on previous round), Ch 8-8.* SCh at last 8 ds.

Round 9: SR 2^2, Ch 10-10. *R 2+2 (to next Ch p on previous round), Ch 10-10.* SCh at last 10 ds.

Round 10: SR 2^2, Ch 12-12. *R 2+2 (to next Ch p on previous round), Ch 12-12.* SCh at last 12 ds.

Round 11: SR 3—3^3—3, Ch 11-11. *R 3—3+3—3 (to next Ch p on previous round), Ch 11-11.* SCh at last 11 ds.

Round 12: SR 2^2, <Ch 12, R 6+6 (to base of next R on previous round), Ch 12>. *R 2+2, <>.* SLJ.

Round 13: SR 6^6, <Ch 13, R 6+6 (to base of next R on previous round), Ch 13>. *R 6+6, <>.* SLJ.

Round 14: SR 6^6, <Ch 14, R 3—3+3—3, (to base of next R on previous round) Ch 14>. *R 6+6, <>.* SLJ.

Round 15: SR 6^6, <Ch 15, R 6+6 (to base of next R on previous round), Ch 15>. *R 6+6, <>.* SLJ.

Round 16: SR 6^6, <Ch 16, R 6+6 (to base of next R on previous round), Ch 16>. *R 6+6, <>.* SLJ.

Round 17: SR 6ˆ6, <Ch 17, R 3—3+3—3 (to base of next R on previous round), Ch 17>. *R 6+6, <>.* SLJ.

Round 18: SR 6ˆ6, <Ch 18, R 6+6 (to base of next R on previous round), Ch 18>. *R 6+6, <>.* SLJ.

Round 19: SR 6ˆ6, <Ch 19, R 6+6 (to base of next R on previous round), Ch 19>. *R 6+6, <>.* SLJ.

Round 20: *R 3—3+3—3 (to base of any main R on previous round), Ch 8-6-6-6-6-8.* SCh at last 8 ds.

Round 21: SR 3ˆ3, <Ch 3, R 6+6 (to base of next R on previous round), Ch 3, *R 3+3 (to next Ch p), Ch 4-4,* repeat * * 3 more times>. ***R 3+3, <>.*** SCh at last 4 ds.

Round 22: SR 3ˆ3, <Ch 3, R 7+7 (to base of next R on previous round), Ch 4, R 7+7 (to same R base), Ch 3, *R 3+3, Ch 4-4,* repeat * * 2 more times>. ***R 3+3, <>.*** SCh at last 4 ds.

Round 23: SR 3ˆ3, <Ch 5, R 9+9 (to base of next R on previous round), Ch 12, R 9+9, Ch 5, *R 3+3, Ch 4-4,* repeat * * 1 more time>. ***R 3+3, <>.*** SCh at last 4 ds.

Round 24: SR 3ˆ3, <Ch 5, R 11+11 (to base of next R on previous round), Ch 6 [Sh2: JR 10] 6, R 11+11 (over Ch between 2 Rs), Ch 6 [Sh2: JR 10] 6, R 11+11, Ch 5, R 3+3, Ch 4-4>. ***R 3+3, <>.*** SCh at last 4 ds.

Round 25: SR 3ˆ3, <Ch 5, R 12+12 (to base of next R on previous round), Ch 6 [Sh2: JR 10] 6, R 13+13, Ch 5 [Sh2: JR 10] 5, R 13+13 (to same R base), Ch 6 [Sh2: JR 10] 6, R 12+12, Ch 5>. ***R 3+3, <>.*** SLJ.

Note: The doily in these photos was tatted without the SR technique. When tatted with the SR technique, as in the instructions, each SR will show two colors.

Cornelia Doily 1

MATERIALS

2 tatting shuttles

DMC Cebelia, size 30

SIZE

6.25 inches

INSTRUCTIONS

Round 1: R 1 X 18 (——— or 5/16 inch p), close R, make last p with Lock Stitch with Sh2. Total 18 ps.

Round 2: *Ch 2-2+ (to next p on previous round).* SCh at last 2 ds.

Round 3: SR 5ˆ5, Ch 3 [Sh2: JR 7] 3. *R 5+5 (to next Ch p on previous round), Ch 3 [Sh2: JR 7] 3.* SLJ.

Round 4: SR 5ˆ5, Ch 8. *R 5+5 (to base of next R on previous round), Ch 8.* SLJ.

Round 5: SR 5ˆ5, Ch 10. *R 5+5 (to base of next R on previous round), Ch 10.* SLJ.

Round 6: SR 5ˆ5, Ch 12. *R 5+5 (to base of next R on previous round), Ch 12.* SLJ.

Round 7: SR 5ˆ5, Ch 14. *R 5+5 (to base of next R on previous round), Ch 14.* SLJ.

Round 8: SR 5ˆ5, Ch 16. *R 5+5 (to base of next R on previous round), Ch 16.* SLJ.

Round 9: SR 5ˆ5, Ch 18. *R 5+5 (to base of next R on previous round), Ch 18.* SLJ.

Round 10: SR 5ˆ5, Ch 20. *R 5+5 (to base of next R on previous round), Ch 20.* SLJ.

Round 11: SR 5ˆ5, Ch 22. *R 5+5 (to base of next R on previous round), Ch 22.* SLJ.

Round 12: SR 5ˆ5, Ch 24. *R 5+5 (to base of next R on previous round), Ch 24.* SLJ.

Round 13: SR 5ˆ5, Ch 26. *R 5+5 (to base of next R on previous round), Ch 26.* SLJ.

Round 14: SR 5ˆ5, <Ch 4, R 5+5 (to same R base on previous round), Ch 13-13>. *R 5+5, <>.* SLJ.

Round 15: SR 5ˆ5, <Ch 4, R 5+5 (over Ch between 2 Rs on previous round), Ch 4, R 5+5, Ch 9+ (to Ch p), make a small MP (-), Ch 9>. *R 5+5, <>.* SLJ.

Round 16: SR 5ˆ5, <Ch 4, R 5+5 (over Ch between 2 Rs on previous round), Ch 4, R 5+5, Ch 4, R

5+5 (over Ch), Ch 4, R 5+5, Ch 7+ (to small MP), make a small MP (-), Ch 7>. *R 5+5, <>.* SLJ.

Round 17: SR 5ˆ5, <Ch 5 [Sh2: JR 10] 5, R 5+5 (to base of 3rd R on previous round), Ch 5 [Sh2: JR 10] 5, R 5+5 (to base of 5th R), Ch 10+ (to small MP) 10>. *R 5+5, <>.* SLJ.

Cornelia Doily 2

MATERIALS

2 tatting shuttles

DMC Cebelia, size 30

SIZE

10.5 inches

INSTRUCTIONS

Round 1: R 1 X 18 (——— or 5/16 inch p), close R, make last p with Lock Stitch with Sh2. Total 18 ps.

Round 2: *Ch 2-2+ (to next p on previous round).* SCh at last 2 ds.

Round 3: SR 5^5, Ch 3 [Sh2: JR 7] 3. *R 5+5 (to next Ch p on previous round), Ch 3 [Sh2: JR 7] 3.* SLJ.

Round 4: SR 5^5, Ch 8. *R 5+5 (to base of next R on previous round), Ch 8.* SLJ.

Round 5: SR 5^5, Ch 10. *R 5+5 (to base of next R on previous round), Ch 10.* SLJ.

Round 6: SR 5^5, Ch 12. *R 5+5 (to base of next R on previous round), Ch 12.* SLJ.

Round 7: SR 5^5, Ch 14. *R 5+5 (to base of next R on previous round), Ch 14.* SLJ.

Round 8: SR 5^5, Ch 16. *R 5+5 (to base of next R on previous round), Ch 16.* SLJ.

Round 9: SR 5^5, Ch 18. *R 5+5 (to base of next R on previous round), Ch 18.* SLJ.

Round 10: SR 5^5, Ch 20. *R 5+5 (to base of next R on previous round), Ch 20.* SLJ.

Round 11: SR 5^5, Ch 22. *R 5+5 (to base of next R on previous round), Ch 22.* SLJ.

Round 12: SR 5^5, Ch 24. *R 5+5 (to base of next R on previous round), Ch 24.* SLJ.

Round 13: SR 5^5, Ch 26. *R 5+5 (to base of next R on previous round), Ch 26.* SLJ.

Round 14: SR 5^5, <Ch 4, R 5+5 (to same R base on previous round), Ch 13-13>. *R 5+5, <>.* SLJ.

Round 15: SR 5^5, <Ch 4, R 5+5 (over Ch between 2 Rs on previous round), Ch 4, R 5+5, Ch 9+ (to Ch p), make a small MP (-), Ch 9>. *R 5+5, <>.* SLJ.

Round 16: SR 5^5, <Ch 4, R 5+5 (over Ch between 2 Rs on previous round), Ch 4, R 5+5, Ch 4, R

5+5 (over Ch), Ch 4, R 5+5, Ch 7+ (to small MP), make a small MP (-), Ch 7>. *R 5+5, <>.* SLJ.

Round 17: SR 5^5, <Ch 5 [Sh2: JR 10] 5, R 5+5 (to base of 3rd R on previous round), Ch 5 [Sh2: JR 10] 5, R 5+5 (to base of 5th R), Ch 10+ (to small MP) 10>. *R 5+5, <>.* SLJ.

Round 18: SR 5^5, <Ch 4-4-4-4-4-4-4, R 5+5 (to next main R base on previous round), Ch 10>. *R 5+5, <>.* SLJ.

Round 19: SR 5^5, <Ch 4, *R 3+3 (to Ch p on previous round), Ch 3-3,* repeat * * 4 more times, R 3+3, Ch 4, R 5+5 (to next main R base), Ch 5>. ***R 5+5, <>.*** SLJ.

Round 20: SR 5^5, <Ch 6, *R 3+3 (to Ch p on previous round), Ch 3-3,* repeat * * 3 more times, R 3+3, Ch 6, R 5+5 (to next main R base), Ch 1-1>. ***R 5+5, <>.*** SCh at last 1 ds.

Round 21: SR 8^8, <Ch 10, *R 3+3 (to Ch p on previous round), Ch 3-3,* repeat * * 2 more times, R 3+3, Ch 10>. ***R 8+8, <>.*** SLJ.

Round 22: SR 12^12, <Ch 3-3, R 12+12 (to same R base on previous round), Ch 12, *R 3+3, Ch 3-3,* repeat * * 1 more time, R 3+3, Ch 12>. ***R 12+12, <>.*** SLJ.

Round 23: SR 13^13, <Ch 8, R 13+13 (to Ch p between two Rs on previous round), Ch 8, R 13+13, Ch 6 [Sh2: JR 7] 6, R 3+3, Ch 3-3, R 3+3, Ch 6 [Sh2: JR 7] 6>. *R 13+13, <>.* SLJ.

Round 24: SR 14^14, <Ch 9 [Sh2: JR 10] 9, R 15+15 (to next R base on previous round), Sh2: R 5—5—5—5—5—5, Ch 9 [Sh2: JR 10] 9, R 14+14, Ch 7 [Sh2: JR 10] 7, R 3+3, Ch 7 [Sh2: JR 10] 7>. *R 14+14, <>.* SLJ.

Alice Motif

MATERIALS

2 tatting shuttles

Lizbeth, size 40

SIZE

2 inches

INSTRUCTIONS

Round 1: R 6-4—4-6, Ch 4 [Sh2: JR 10] 3, Sh2: R 3—3—3—3—3—3, Ch 4 [Sh2: JR 10] 3. *R 6+4—4-6, Ch 4 [Sh2: JR 10] 3, Sh2: R 3—3—3—3—3—3, Ch 4 [Sh2: JR 10] 3.* Repeat * * 10 more times. Total 12 Rs and Chs. SLJ.

Note: Refer to the photo for the direction of the chains.

Alice Doily 1

MATERIALS

2 tatting shuttles

Lizbeth, size 40

SIZE

3.5 inches

INSTRUCTIONS

Round 1: R 6-4—4-6, Ch 4 [Sh2: JR 10] 3, Sh2: R 3—3—3—3—3—3, Ch 4 [Sh2: JR 10] 3. *R 6+4—4-6, Ch 4 [Sh2: JR 10] 3, Sh2: R 3—3—3—3—3—3, Ch 4 [Sh2: JR 10] 3.* Repeat * * 10 more times. Total 12 Rs and Chs. SLJ.

Note: Refer to the photo for the direction of the chains.

Round 2: *R 3—3—3+3—3—3 (to any middle R p on previous round), Ch 5 [Sh2: JR 10] 5 [Sh2: JR 10] 5 [Sh2: R 3—3—3—3—3—3—3—3] 5 [Sh2: JR 10] 5 [Sh2: JR 10] 5.* SLJ.

Alice Doily 2

MATERIALS

2 tatting shuttles

Lizbeth, size 40

SIZE

10 inches

INSTRUCTIONS

Round 1: R 6-4—4-6, Ch 4 [Sh2: JR 10] 3, Sh2: R 3—3—3—3—3—3, Ch 4 [Sh2: JR 10] 3. *R 6+4—4-6, Ch 4 [Sh2: JR 10] 3, Sh2: R 3—3—3—3—3—3, Ch 4 [Sh2: JR 10] 3.* Repeat * * 10 more times. Total 12 Rs and Chs. SLJ.

Note: Refer to the photo for the direction of the chains.

Round 2: *R 3—3—3+3—3—3—3 (to any middle R p on previous round), Ch 5 [Sh2: JR 10] 5 [Sh2: JR 10] 5 [Sh2: R 3—3—3—3—3—3—3—3] 5 [Sh2: JR 10] 5 [Sh2: JR 10] 5.* SLJ.

Round 3: *R 3—3—3—3+3—3—3—3 (to any middle R p on previous round), Ch 4-4-4-4-4-4-4-4-4-4-4.* SCh at last 4 ds.

Round 4: SR 3ˆ3, <Ch 3 [Sh2: JR 10] 3, *R 3+3 (to next Ch p on previous round), Ch 3-3,* repeat * * 8 more times>. ***R 3+3, <>.*** SCh at last 3 ds.

Round 5: SR 3ˆ3, <Ch 3 [Sh2: JR 10] 3, *R 3+3 (to next Ch p on previous round), Ch 3-3,* repeat * * 7 more times>. ***R 3+3, <>.*** SCh at last 3 ds.

Round 6: SR 3ˆ3, <Ch 4 [Sh2: JR 10] 4, *R 3+3 (to next Ch p on previous round), Ch 3-3,* repeat * * 6 more times>.***R 3+3, <>.*** SCh at last 3 ds.

Round 7: SR 3ˆ3, <Ch 4 [Sh2: JR 10] 4 [Sh2: JR 10] 4, *R 3+3 (to next Ch p on previous round), Ch 3-3,* repeat * * 5 more times>. ***R 3+3, <>.*** SCh at last 3 ds.

Round 8: SR 3ˆ3, <Ch 6 [Sh2: JR 10] 6 [Sh2: JR 10] 6, *R 3+3 (to next Ch p on previous round), Ch 3-3,* repeat * * 4 more times>. ***R 3+3, <>.*** SCh at last 3 ds.

Round 9: SR 3^3, <Ch 7 [Sh2: JR 10] 7 [Sh2: JR 10] 7 [Sh2: JR 10] 7, *R 3+3 (to next Ch p on previous round), Ch 4-4,* repeat * * 3 more times>. ***R 3+3, <>.*** SCh at last 4 ds.

Round 10: SR 3^3, <Ch 8 [Sh2: JR 10] 8 [Sh2: JR 10] 8[Sh2: JR 10] 8 [Sh2: JR 10] 8, *R 3+3 (to next Ch p on previous round), Ch 4-4,* repeat * * 2 more times>. ***R 3+3, <>.*** SCh at last 4 ds.

Round 11: SR 3^3, <Ch 3 [Sh2: JR 10] 3, R 3+3 (to JR on previous round), Ch 6 [Sh2: JR 10] 6, R 3+3, Ch 7 [Sh2: JR 10] 7, R 3+3, Ch 6 [Sh2: JR 10] 6, R 3+3, Ch 3 [Sh2: JR 10] 3, *R 3+3 (to next Ch p), Ch 4-4,* repeat * * 1 more time>. ***R 3+3, <>.*** SCh at last 4 ds.

Round 12: SR 3^3, <Ch 2 [Sh2: JR 10] 2, R 3+3 (to JR on previous round), Ch 6 [Sh2: JR 10] 6, R 3+3, Ch 9 [Sh2: JR 10] 9, R 3+3, Ch 9 [Sh2: JR 10] 9, R 3+3, Ch 6 [Sh2: JR 10] 6, R 3+3, Ch 2 [Sh2: JR 10] 2, R 3+3 (to next Ch p), Ch 4-4>. *R 3+3, <>.* SCh at last 4 ds.

Round 13: SR 3^3, <Ch 2 [Sh2: JR 10] 2, R 3+3 (to JR on previous round), Ch 3 [Sh2: JR 10] 3, R 3+3, Ch 10 [Sh2: JR 10] 10, R 3+3, Ch 7 [Sh2: JR 10] 7 [Sh2: JR 10] 7 [Sh2: JR 10] 7, R 3+3, Ch 10 [Sh2: JR 10] 10, R 3+3, Ch 3 [Sh2: JR 10] 3, R 3+3, Ch 2 [Sh2: JR 10] 2>. *R 3+3, <>.* SLJ.

Lavender Doily 1

MATERIALS

2 tatting shuttles

DMC Cordonnet, size 30

SIZE

7 inches

INSTRUCTIONS

Round 1: R 1 X 18 (———— or 1/2 inch p), close R, make last p with Lock Stitch with Sh 2. Total 18 ps.

Round 2: *Ch 3-3+ (to next p on previous round).* SCh at last 3 ds.

Round 3: SR 2ˆ2, Ch 4-4. *R 2+2 (to next Ch p on previous round), Ch 4-4.* SCh at last 4 ds.

Round 4: SR 2ˆ2, Ch 6-6. *R 2+2 (to next Ch p on previous round), Ch 6-6.* SCh at last 6 ds.

Round 5: SR 2ˆ2, Ch 8-8. *R 2+2 (to next Ch p on previous round), Ch 8-8.* SCh at last 8 ds.

Round 6: SR 2ˆ2, <Ch 5 [Sh2: JR 10] 5-5 [Sh2: JR 10] 5>. *R 2+2 (to next Ch p on previous round), <>.* SCh at last 10 ds.

Round 7: SR 2ˆ2, <Ch 6 [Sh2: JR 10] 6-6 [Sh2: JR 10] 6>. *R 2+2 (to next Ch p on previous round), <>.* SCh at last 12 ds.

Round 8: SR 2ˆ2, <Ch 4-4-4-4-4-4>. *R 2+2 (to next Ch p on previous round), <>.* SCh at last 4 ds.

Round 9: SR 2ˆ2, <*R 2+2 (to next Ch p on previous round), Ch 3-3,* repeat * * 4 more times>. ***R 2+2, <>.*** SCh at last 3 ds.

Round 10: SR 2ˆ2, <*R 2+2 (to next Ch p on previous round), Ch 4-4,* repeat * * 3 more times>. ***R 2+2, <>.*** SCh at last 4 ds.

Round 11: SR 2ˆ2, <*R 2+2 (to next Ch p on previous round), Ch 5-5,* repeat * * 2 more times>. ***R 2+2, <>.*** SCh at last 5 ds.

Round 12: SR 2ˆ2, <Ch 4 [Sh2: JR 10] 4, *R 2+2 (to next Ch p on previous round), Ch 6-6,* repeat *
* 1 more time>. ***R 2+2, <>.*** SCh at last 6 ds.

Round 13: SR 2ˆ2, <Ch 5 [Sh2: JR 10] 5 [Sh2: JR 10] 5 [Sh2: JR 10] 5, R 2+2 (to next Ch p on
previous round), Ch 16>. *R 2+2, <>.* SLJ.

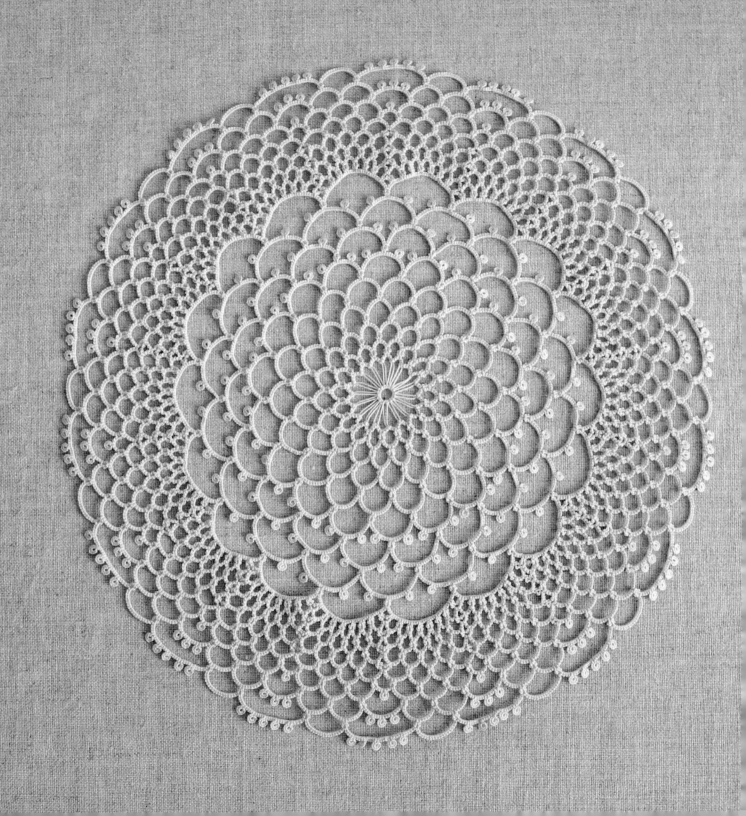

Lavender Doily 2

MATERIALS

2 tatting shuttles

DMC Cordonnet, size 30

SIZE

9.5 inches

INSTRUCTIONS

Round 1: R 1 X 18 (———— or 1/2 inch p), close R, make last p with Lock Stitch with Sh 2. Total 18 ps.

Round 2: *Ch 3-3+ (to next p on previous round).* SCh at last 3 ds.

Round 3: SR 2^2, Ch 4-4. *R 2+2 (to next Ch p on previous round), Ch 4-4.* SCh at last 4 ds.

Round 4: SR 2^2, Ch 6-6. *R 2+2 (to next Ch p on previous round), Ch 6-6.* SCh at last 6 ds.

Round 5: SR 2^2, Ch 8-8. *R 2+2 (to next Ch p on previous round), Ch 8-8.* SCh at last 8 ds.

Round 6: SR 2^2, Ch 10-10. *R 2+2 (to next Ch p on previous round), Ch 10-10.* SCh at last 10 ds.

Round 7: SR 2^2, <Ch 6 [Sh2: JR 10] 6-6 [Sh2: JR 10] 6>. *R 2+2 (to next Ch p on previous round), <>.* SCh at last 12 ds.

Round 8: SR 2^2, <Ch 7 [Sh2: JR 10] 7-7 [Sh2: JR 10] 7>. *R 2+2 (to next Ch p on previous round), <>.* SCh at last 14 ds.

Round 9: SR 2^2, <Ch 8 [Sh2: JR 10] 8-8 [Sh2: JR 10] 8>. *R 2+2 (to next Ch p on previous round), <>.* SCh at last 16 ds.

Round 10: SR 2^2, <Ch 4-4-4-4-4-4-4-4-4>. *R 2+2 (to next Ch p on previous round), <>.* SCh at last 4 ds.

Round 11: SR 2^2, <*R 2+2 (to next Ch p on previous round), Ch 3-3,* repeat * * 6 more times>. ***R 2+2, <>.*** SCh at last 3 ds.

Round 12: SR 2^2, <*R 2+2 (to next Ch p on previous round), Ch 3-3,* repeat * * 5 more times>.

R 2+2, <>. SCh at last 3 ds.

Round 13: SR 2ˆ2, <*R 2+2 (to next Ch p on previous round), Ch 4-4,* repeat * * 4 more times>. ***R 2+2, <>.*** SCh at last 4 ds.

Round 14: SR 2ˆ2, <*R 2+2 (to next Ch p on previous round), Ch 5-5,* repeat * * 3 more times>. ***R 2+2, <>.*** SCh at last 5 ds.

Round 15: SR 2ˆ2, <Ch 3 [Sh2: JR 10] 3, *R 2+2 (to next Ch p on previous round), Ch 6-6,* repeat * * 2 more times>. ***R 2+2, <>.*** SCh at last 6 ds.

Round 16: SR 2ˆ2, <Ch 4 [Sh2: JR 10] 4 [Sh2: JR 10] 4 [Sh2: JR 10] 4, *R 2+2 (to next Ch p on previous round), Ch 8-8,* repeat * * 1 more time>. ***R 2+2, <>.*** SCh at last 8 ds.

Round 17: SR 2ˆ2, <Ch 5 [Sh2: JR 10] 5 [Sh2: JR 10] 5 [Sh2: JR 10] 5 [Sh2: JR 10] 5 [Sh2: JR 10] 5, R 2+2 (to next Ch p on previous round), Ch 18>. *R 2+2, <>.* SLJ.

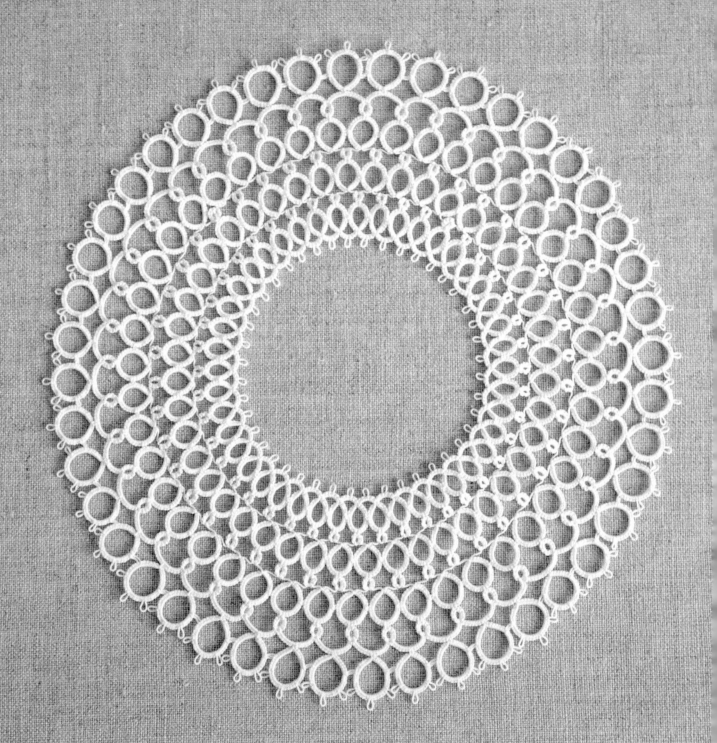

Chamomile Doily 1

MATERIALS

2 tatting shuttles

DMC Cebelia, size 30

SIZE

7.5 inches

INSTRUCTIONS

Round 1: R 5-6-6-5, Ch 3—3. *R 5+6-6-5, Ch 3—3.* Repeat * * 42 more times. Total 44 Rs and Chs. SLJ.

Round 2: R 3+3 (to any R p on previous round), leave 1/8 inch thread, RW, R 6-7-7-6, leave 1/8 inch thread, RW. *R 3+3, leave 1/8 inch thread, RW, R 6+7-7-6, leave 1/8 inch thread, RW.* SLJ.

Round 3: R 4+4 (to any R p on previous round), leave 3/16 inch thread, RW, R 7--8-8--7, leave 3/16 inch thread, RW. *R 4+4, leave 3/16 inch thread, RW, R 7+8-8--7, leave 3/16 inch thread, RW.* SLJ.

Round 4: R 5+5 (to any R p on previous round), Ch 7 [Sh2: R 7—6—6—6—6—7] 7. *R 5+5, Ch 7 [Sh2: R 7+6—6—6—6—7] 7.* SLJ.

Chamomile Doily 2

MATERIALS

2 tatting shuttles

DMC Cebelia, size 30

SIZE

7.5 inches

INSTRUCTIONS

Round 1: R 5-6-6-5, Ch 3—3. *R 5+6-6-5, Ch 3—3.* Repeat * * 42 more times. Total 44 Rs and Chs. SLJ.

Round 2: R 3+3 (to any R p on previous round), leave 1/8 inch thread, RW, R 6-7-7-6, leave 1/8 inch thread, RW. *R 3+3, leave 1/8 inch thread, RW, R 6+7-7-6, leave 1/8 inch thread, RW.* SLJ.

Round 3: R 4+4 (to any R p on previous round), leave 3/16 inch thread, RW, R 7--8-8--7, leave 3/16 inch thread, RW. *R 4+4, leave 3/16 inch thread, RW, R 7+8-8--7, leave 3/16 inch thread, RW.* SLJ.

Round 4: R 5+5 (to any R p on previous round), Ch 7 [Sh2: {R 8—4-4, R 4+5—4—4—4—4—5-4, R 4+4—8}] 7, R 5+5, Ch 7 [Sh2: R 4+4—4—4] 7. *R 5+5, Ch 7 [Sh2: {R 8+4-4, R 4+5—4—4—4—4—5-4, R 4+4—8}] 7, R 5+5, Ch 7 [Sh2: R 4+4—4—4] 7.* SLJ.

Evangeline Doily 1

MATERIALS

2 tatting shuttles

DMC Cebelia, size 30

SIZE

7 inches

INSTRUCTIONS

Round 1: R 3 X 25 (-). Total 24 ps.

Round 2: *Ch 5/5, 5/5, 5/5, 5/5-1, 3/5, 5/5, 5/5, 5/5+ (to next p on previous round).* SLJ.

Round 3: Attach both threads to any Ch p on previous round. *Ch 4-4+ (to next Ch p).* SCh at last 4 ds.

Round 4: *Ch 5-5+ (to next Ch p on previous round).* SCh at last 5 ds.

Round 5: *Ch 6-6+ (to next Ch p on previous round).* SCh at last 6 ds.

Round 6: *Ch 7-7+ (to next Ch p on previous round).* SCh at last 7 ds.

Round 7: *Ch 8-8+ (to next Ch p on previous round).* SCh at last 8 ds.

Round 8: *Ch 9-9+ (to next Ch p on previous round).* SCh at last 9 ds.

Round 9: *Ch 5 [Sh2: JR 12] 5-Ch 5 [Sh2: JR 12] 5+ (to next Ch p on previous round).* SCh at last 10 ds.

Round 10: *Ch 5 [Sh2: JR 12] 6-Ch 6 [Sh2: JR 12] 5+ (to next Ch p on previous round).* SCh at last 11 ds.

Round 11: *Ch 6 [Sh2: JR 12] 6-Ch 6 [Sh2: JR 12] 6+ (to next Ch p on previous round).* SCh at last 12 ds.

Round 12: *Ch 6 [Sh2: JR 12] 7-Ch 7 [Sh2: JR 12] 6+ (to next Ch p on previous round).* SCh at last 13 ds.

Round 13: *Ch 7 [Sh2: JR 12] 7-Ch 7 [Sh2: JR 12] 7+ (to next Ch p on previous round).* SCh at last

14 ds.

Round 14: *Ch 7 [Sh2: JR 12] 8 [Sh2: JR 12] 8 [Sh2: JR 12] 7+ (to next Ch p on previous round).* SLJ.

Note: Instead of making SCh from rounds 2 to 14, the last chains can be tatted in the regular way and then SLJ.

Evangeline Doily 2

MATERIALS

2 tatting shuttles

DMC Cebelia, size 30

SIZE

11 inches

INSTRUCTIONS

Round 1: R 3 X 25 (-). Total 24 ps.

Round 2: *Ch 5/5, 5/5, 5/5, 5/5-1, 3/5, 5/5, 5/5, 5/5+ (to next p on previous round).* SLJ.

Round 3: Attach both threads to any Ch p on previous round. *Ch 4-4+ (to next Ch p).* SCh at last 4 ds.

Round 4: *Ch 5-5+ (to next Ch p on previous round).* SCh at last 5 ds.

Round 5: *Ch 6-6+ (to next Ch p on previous round).* SCh at last 6 ds.

Round 6: *Ch 7-7+ (to next Ch p on previous round).* SCh at last 7 ds.

Round 7: *Ch 8-8+ (to next Ch p on previous round).* SCh at last 8 ds.

Round 8: *Ch 9-9+ (to next Ch p on previous round).* SCh at last 9 ds.

Round 9: *Ch 5 [Sh2: JR 12] 5-Ch 5 [Sh2: JR 12] 5+ (to next Ch p on previous round).* SCh at last 10 ds.

Round 10: *Ch 5 [Sh2: JR 12] 6-Ch 6 [Sh2: JR 12] 5+ (to next Ch p on previous round).* SCh at last 11 ds.

Round 11: *Ch 6 [Sh2: JR 12] 6-Ch 6 [Sh2: JR 12] 6+ (to next Ch p on previous round).* SCh at last 12 ds.

Round 12: *Ch 6 [Sh2: JR 12] 7-Ch 7 [Sh2: JR 12] 6+ (to next Ch p on previous round).* SCh at last 13 ds.

Round 13: *Ch 7 [Sh2: JR 12] 7-Ch 7 [Sh2: JR 12] 7+ (to next Ch p on previous round).* SCh at last

14 ds.

Round 14: *Ch 7 [Sh2: JR 10] 8-Ch 8 [Sh2: JR 10] 7+ (to next Ch p on previous round).* SCh at last 15 ds.

Round 15: SR 5—5^5—5, Ch 6-6-6-6-6. *R 5—5+5—5 (to next Ch p on previous round), Ch 6-6-6-6-6.* SCh at last 6 ds.

Round 16: ***Ch 4, R 6+6 (to base of next R on previous round), Ch 4+ (to next Ch p), *Ch 4-4+,* repeat * * 2 more times, Ch 6-6+, *Ch 4-4+,* repeat * * 2 more times.*** SCh at last 4 ds.

Round 17: ***Ch 7, R 7+7 (to base of next R on previous round), Ch 7+ (to next Ch p), *Ch 4-4+,* repeat * * 5 more times.*** SCh at last 4 ds.

Round 18: ***Ch 12, R 8+8 (to base of next R on previous round), Ch 12+ (to next Ch p), *Ch 4-4+,* repeat * * 4 more times.*** SCh at last 4 ds.

Round 19: ***Ch 14, R 8+8 (to base of next R on previous round), Ch 10, R 8+8 (to same R base), Ch 14+ (to next Ch p), *Ch 4-4+,* repeat * * 3 more times.*** SCh at last 4 ds.

Round 20: ***Ch 8 [Sh2: JR 12] 8, R 8+8 (to base of next R on previous round), Ch 24, R 8+8, Ch 8 [Sh2: JR 12] 8+ (to next Ch p), *Ch 4-4+,* repeat * * 2 more times.*** SCh at last 4 ds.

Round 21: ***Ch 18, R 8+8 (to base of next R on previous round), Ch 15 [Sh2: JR 12] 10 [Sh2: JR 12] 15, R 8+8, Ch 18+ (to next Ch p), *Ch 4-4+,* repeat * * 1 more time.*** SCh at last 4 ds.

Round 22: *Ch 10 [Sh2: JR 12] 10, R 8+8 (to base of next R on previous round), Ch 20, R 3+3 (to JR), Ch 6 [Sh2: JR 12] 6, R 3+3, Ch 20, R 8+8, Ch 10 [Sh2: JR 12] 10+ (to next Ch p), Ch 4 [Sh2: JR 12] 4+.* SLJ.

Note: Instead of making SCh from rounds 2 to 14, the last chains can be tatted in the regular way and then SLJ.

Elizabeth Motif

MATERIALS

2 tatting shuttles

DMC Cebelia, size 30

SIZE

2.25 inches

INSTRUCTIONS

Round 1: R 1 X 12 (——— or 3/8 inch p), close R, make last p with Lock Stitch with Sh 2. Total 12 ps.

Round 2: *Ch 3-3+ (to next p on previous round).* SCh at last 3 ds.

Round 3: SR 8ˆ8, <Ch 6 [Sh2: JR 10] 6>. *R 8+8 (to next Ch p on previous round), <>.* SLJ.

Round 4: SR 8ˆ8, Ch 10—10. *R 8+8 (to base of next R on previous round), Ch 10—10.* SLJ.

Elizabeth Doily 1

MATERIALS

2 tatting shuttles

DMC Cebelia, size 30

SIZE

4.5 inches

INSTRUCTIONS

Round 1: R 1 X 12 (——— or 3/8 inch p), close R, make last p with Lock Stitch with Sh 2. Total 12 ps.

Round 2: *Ch 3-3+ (to next p on previous round).* SCh at last 3 ds.

Round 3: SR 8ˆ8, <Ch 6 [Sh2: JR 10] 6>. *R 8+8 (to next Ch p on previous round), <>.* SLJ.

Round 4: SR 8ˆ8, Ch 10-10. *R 8+8 (to base of next R on previous round), Ch 10-10.* SLJ.

Round 5: SR 8ˆ8, <Ch 10+ (to next Ch p on previous round), make a small MP (-), Ch 10>. *R 8+8 (to base of next R), <>.* SLJ.

Round 6: SR 8ˆ8, <Ch 6 [Sh2: JR 10] 6, R 8+8 (to small MP on previous round), Ch 6 [Sh2: JR 10] 6>. *R 8+8 (to base of next R), <>.* SLJ.

Round 7: SR 8ˆ8, <Ch 7 [Sh 2: JR 10] 7>. *R 8+8 (to base of next R on previous round), <>.* SLJ.

Round 8: SR 16ˆ16, <Ch 9 [Sh2: JR 10] 9>. *R 16+16 (to base of next R on previous round), <>.* SLJ.

Elizabeth Doily 2

MATERIALS

2 tatting shuttles

DMC Cebelia, size 30

SIZE

7.5 inches

INSTRUCTIONS

Round 1: R 1 X 12 (——— or 3/8 inch p), close R, make last p with Lock Stitch with Sh 2. Total 12 ps.

Round 2: *Ch 3-3 + (to next p on previous round).* SCh at last 3 ds.

Round 3: SR 8ˆ8, <Ch 6 [Sh2: JR 10] 6>. *R 8+8 (to next Ch p on previous round), <>.* SLJ.

Round 4: SR 8ˆ8, Ch 10-10. *R 8+8 (to base of next R on previous round), Ch 10-10.* SLJ.

Round 5: SR 8ˆ8, <Ch 10+ (to next Ch p on previous round), make a small MP (-), Ch 10>. *R 8+8 (to base of next R), <>.* SLJ.

Round 6: SR 8ˆ8, <Ch 6 [Sh2: JR 10] 6, R 8+8 (to small MP on previous round), Ch 6 [Sh2: JR 10] 6>. *R 8+8 (to base of next R), <>.* SLJ.

Round 7: SR 8ˆ8, <Ch 7 [Sh2: JR 10] 7>. *R 8+8 (to base of next R on previous round), <>.* SLJ.

Round 8: SR 16ˆ16, <Ch 9 [Sh2: JR 10] 9>. *R 16+16 (to base of next R on previous round), <>.* SLJ.

Round 9: SR 8ˆ8, <Ch 10 [Sh2: JR 10] 10>. *R 8+8 (to base of next R on previous round), <>.* SLJ.

Round 10: SR 18ˆ18, Ch 12-12. *R 18+18 (to base of next R on previous round), Ch 12-12.* SLJ.

Round 11: SR 8ˆ8, <Ch 13, R 2+2 (to next Ch p on previous round), Ch 13>. *R 8+8 (to base of next R), <>.* SLJ.

Round 12: SR 8ˆ8, <Ch 7 [Sh2: JR 10] 7>. *R 8+8 (to base of next R on previous round), <>.* SLJ.

Round 13: SR 8ˆ8, <Ch 8 [Sh2: JR 10] 8>. *R 8+8 (to base of next R on previous round), <>.* SLJ.

Elizabeth Doily 3

MATERIALS

2 tatting shuttles

DMC Cebelia, size 30

SIZE

11.5 inches

INSTRUCTIONS

Round 1: R 1 X 12 (——— or 3/8 inch p), close R, make last p with Lock Stitch with Sh 2. Total 12 ps.

Round 2: *Ch 3-3 + (to next p on previous round).* SCh at last 3 ds.

Round 3: SR 8^8, <Ch 6 [Sh2: JR 10] 6>. *R 8+8 (to next Ch p on previous round), <>.* SLJ.

Round 4: SR 8^8, Ch 10-10. *R 8+8 (to base of next R on previous round), Ch 10-10.* SLJ.

Round 5: SR 8^8, <Ch 10+ (to next Ch p on previous round), make a small MP (-), Ch 10>. *R 8+8 (to next R base), <>.* SLJ.

Round 6: SR 8^8, <Ch 6 [Sh2: JR 10] 6, R 8+8 (to small MP on previous round), Ch 6 [Sh2: JR 10] 6>. *R 8+8 (to base of next R), <>.* SLJ.

Round 7: SR 8^8, <Ch 7 [Sh2: JR 10] 7>. *R 8+8 (to base of next R on previous round), <>.* SLJ.

Round 8: SR 16^16, <Ch 9 [Sh2: JR 10] 9>. *R 16+16 (to base of next R on previous round), <>.* SLJ.

Round 9: SR 8^8, <Ch 10 [Sh2: JR 10] 10>. *R 8+8 (to base of next R on previous round), <>.* SLJ.

Round 10: SR 18^18, Ch 12-12. *R 18+18 (to base of next R on previous round), Ch 12-12.* SLJ.

Round 11: SR 8^8, <Ch 13, R 2+2 (to next Ch p on previous round), Ch 13>. *R 8+8 (to base of next R), <>.* SLJ.

Round 12: SR 8^8, <Ch 7 [Sh2: JR 10] 7>. *R 8+8 (to base of next R on previous round), <>.* SLJ.

Round 13: SR 8^8, < Ch 8 [Sh2: JR 10] 8>. *R 8+8 (to base of next R on previous round), <>.* SLJ.

Round 14: SR 20^20, <Ch 8-5-5-5-5-8>. *R 20+20 (to base of next R on previous round), <>.* SLJ.

Round 15: SR 8^8 <Ch 7, *R 4+4 (to next Ch p on previous round), Ch 3-3,* repeat * * 3 more times,

R 4+4, Ch 7>. ***R 8+8 (to base of next R), <>.*** SLJ.

Round 16: SR 10ˆ10, <Ch 7, *R 4+4 (to next Ch p on previous round), Ch 3-3,* repeat * * 2 more times, R 4+4, Ch 7, R 10+10 (to base of next R), Ch 7>. ***R 10+10 (to same R base), <>.*** SLJ.

Round 17: SR 12ˆ12, <Ch 7, *R 4+4 (next Ch p on previous round), Ch 3-3,* repeat * * 1 more time, R 4+4, Ch 7, R 12+12 (to base of next R), Ch 9, R 12+12 (over Ch between 2 Rs), Ch 9>. ***R 12+12 (to base of next R), <>.*** SLJ.

Round 18: SR 12ˆ12, <Ch 7, R 4+4 (to next Ch p on previous round), Ch 3-3, R 4+4, Ch 7, R 12+12, Ch 7 [Sh2: JR 10] 7, R 12+12, Ch 7 [Sh2: JR 10] 7>. *R 12+12, <>.* SLJ.

Round 19: SR 12ˆ12, <Ch 7, R 4+4 (to next Ch p on previous round), Ch 7, R 12+12 (to base of next R), Ch 6 [Sh2: JR 10] 6 [Sh2: JR 10] 6 [Sh2: JR 10] 6, R 12+12, Ch 6 [Sh2: JR 10] 6 [Sh2: JR 10] 6 [Sh2: JR 10] 6>. *R 12+12, <>.* SLJ.

Charlotte Doily 1

MATERIALS

2 tatting shuttles

DMC Cordonnet, size 30

SIZE

6.75 inches

INSTRUCTIONS

Round 1: R 4—3—3—4, Ch 4—6—4. *R 4+3—3—4, Ch 4—6—4.* Repeat * * 6 more times. Total 8 Rs & Chs. SCh at last 4 ds.

Round 2: SR 3—-4ˆ3—-4, Ch 4—6—4. *R 4+3+ (to next Ch p on previous round) 3—-4, Ch 4—6—4.* SCh at last 4 ds.

Round 3: SR 3--4ˆ3—4, Ch 5—4—5. *R 4+3+ (to next Ch p on previous round) 3--4, Ch 5—4—5.* SCh at last 5 ds.

Round 4: SR 2ˆ2, Ch 2-2. *R 2+2 (to next Ch p on previous round), Ch 2-2.* SCh at last 2 ds.

Round 5: SR 2ˆ2, Ch 2-2. *R 2+2 (to next Ch p on previous round), Ch 2-2.* SCh at last 2 ds.

Round 6: SR 2ˆ2, Ch 2-2. *R 2+2 (to next Ch p on previous round), Ch 2-2.* SCh at last 2 ds.

Round 7: SR 2ˆ2, Ch 3-3. *R 2+2 (to next Ch p on previous round), Ch 3-3.* SCh at last 3 ds.

Round 8: SR 2ˆ2, Ch 3-3. *R 2+2 (to next Ch p on previous round), Ch 3-3.* SCh at last 3 ds.

Round 9: SR 2ˆ2, Ch 3-3. *R 2+2 (to next Ch p on previous round), Ch 3-3.* SCh at last 3 ds.

Round 10: SR 2ˆ2, Ch 4-4. *R 2+2 (to next Ch p on previous round), Ch 4-4.* SCh at last 4 ds.

Round 11: SR 2ˆ2, Ch 4-4. *R 2+2 (to next Ch p on previous round), Ch 4-4.* SCh at last 4 ds.

Round 12: SR 2ˆ2, Ch 5-5. *R 2+2 (to next Ch p on previous round), Ch 5-5.* SCh at last 5 ds.

Round 13: SR 2ˆ2, Ch 10. *R 2+2 (to next Ch p on previous round), Ch 10.* SLJ.

Charlotte Doily 2

MATERIALS

2 tatting shuttles

DMC Cebelia, size 30

SIZE

12 inches

INSTRUCTIONS

Round 1: R 4—3—3—4, Ch 4—6—4. *R 4+3—3—4, Ch 4—6—4.* Repeat * * 6 more times. Total 8 Rs & Chs. SCh at last 4 ds.

Round 2: SR 3—-4ˆ3—-4, Ch 4—6—4. *R 4+3+ (to next Ch p on previous round) 3—-4, Ch 4—6—4.* SCh at last 4 ds.

Round 3: SR 3--4ˆ3--4, Ch 5—4—5. *R 4+3+ (to next Ch p on previous round) 3--4, Ch 5—4—5.* SCh at last 5 ds.

Round 4: SR 2ˆ2, Ch 2-2. *R 2+2 (to next Ch p on previous round), Ch 2-2.* SCh at last 2 ds.

Round 5: SR 2ˆ2, Ch 2-2. *R 2+2 (to next Ch p on previous round), Ch 2-2.* SCh at last 2 ds.

Round 6: SR 2ˆ2, Ch 2-2. *R 2+2 (to next Ch p on previous round), Ch 2-2.* SCh at last 2 ds.

Round 7: SR 2ˆ2, Ch 3-3. *R 2+2 (to next Ch p on previous round), Ch 3-3.* SCh at last 3 ds.

Round 8: SR 2ˆ2, Ch 3-3. *R 2+2 (to next Ch p on previous round), Ch 3-3.* SCh at last 3 ds.

Round 9: SR 2ˆ2, Ch 3-3. *R 2+2 (to next Ch p on previous round), Ch 3-3.* SCh at last 3 ds.

Round 10: SR 2ˆ2, Ch 4-4. *R 2+2 (to next Ch p on previous round), Ch 4-4.* SCh at last 4 ds.

Round 11: SR 2ˆ2, Ch 4-4. *R 2+2 (to next Ch p on previous round), Ch 4-4.* SCh at last 4 ds.

Round 12: SR 2ˆ2, Ch 5-5. *R 2+2 (to next Ch p on previous round), Ch 5-5.* SCh at last 5 ds.

Round 13: SR 2ˆ2, Ch 5-5. *R 2+2 (to next Ch p on previous round), Ch 5-5.* SCh at last 5 ds.

Round 14: SR 2ˆ2, Ch 6-6. *R 2+2 (to next Ch p on previous round), Ch 6-6.* SCh at last 6 ds.

Round 15: SR 2ˆ2, Ch 6-6. *R 2+2 (to next Ch p on previous round), Ch 6-6.* SCh at last 6 ds.

Round 16: SR 2^2, Ch 7-7. *R 2+2 (to next Ch p on previous round), Ch 7-7.* SCh at last 7 ds.

Round 17: SR 2^2, Ch 7-7. *R 2+2 (to next Ch p on previous round), Ch 7-7.* SCh at last 7 ds.

Round 18: SR 2^2, Ch 8-8. *R 2+2 (to next Ch p on previous round), Ch 8-8.* SCh at last 8 ds.

Round 19: SR 2^2, Ch 8-8. *R 2+2 (to next Ch p on previous round), Ch 8-8.* SCh at last 8 ds.

Round 20: SR 2^2, Ch 9-9. *R 2+2 (to next Ch p on previous round), Ch 9-9.* SCh at last 9 ds.

Round 21: SR 2^2, Ch 9-9. *R 2+2 (to next Ch p on previous round), Ch 9-9.* SCh at last 9 ds.

Round 22: SR 2^2, Ch 10-10. *R 2+2 (to next Ch p on previous round), Ch 10-10.* SCh at last 10 ds.

Round 23: SR 2^2, Ch 20. *R 2+2 (to next Ch p on previous round), Ch 20.* SLJ.

Josephine Doily

MATERIALS

2 tatting shuttles

Lizbeth, size 40

SIZE

11.5 inches

INSTRUCTIONS

Round 1: R 5 X 12 (-). Total 12 ps.

Round 2: Ch 5/5-5/5, 5/5, 5/5-Ch 1, 4/5, 5/5, 5/5-5/5+ (to next p on previous round). *Ch 5/5+5/5, 5/5, 5/5-Ch 1, 4/5, 5/5, 5/5-5/5+.* SLJ.

Round 3: Attach both threads to any p on previous round. *Ch 3/3, 3/3, 3/3-Ch 1, 2/3, 3/3, 3/3+ (to next Ch p).* SLJ.

Round 4: Attach both threads to any p on previous round. *Ch 5/5, 5/5 [Sh2: JR 10] 1, 4/5, 5/5 [Sh2: JR 10] 1, 4/5, 5/5-Ch 1, 4/5, 5/5 [Sh2: JR 12] 1, 4/5, 5/5 [Sh2: JR 10] 1, 4/5, 5/5+ (to next Ch p).* SLJ.

Note: Chains after p in reverse order for rounds 2 through 4.

Round 5: *R 5—5+5—5 (to any Ch p on previous round), Ch 5-6-6-6-6-6-5.* SCh at last 5 ds.

Round 6: SR 4ˆ4, <Ch 3-3, *R 4+4 (to next Ch p on previous round), Ch 3-3,* repeat * * 4 more times>. ***R 4+4, <>.*** SCh at 3 ds.

Round 7: SR 4ˆ4, <Ch 6, R 6+6 (to next Ch p on previous round), Ch 6, *R 4+4, Ch 3-3,* repeat * * 3 more times>. ***R 4+4, <>.*** SCh at last 3 ds.

Round 8: SR 4ˆ4, <Ch 7, R 7+7 (to base of next R on previous round), Ch 6, R 7+7 (to same R base), Ch 7, *R 4+4, Ch 3-3,* repeat * * 2 more times>. ***R 4+4, <>.*** SCh at last 3 ds.

Round 9: SR 4ˆ4, <Ch 9, R 8+8 (to base of next R on previous round), Ch 12, R 8+8, Ch 9, *R 4+4, Ch 3-3,* repeat * * 1 more time>. ***R 4+4, <>.*** SCh at last 3 ds.

Round 10: SR 4^4, <Ch 12, R 9+9 (to base of next R on previous round), Ch 6 [Sh2: JR 10] 9 [Sh2: JR 10] 6, R 9+9, Ch 12, R 4+4, Ch 3-3>. *R 4+4, <>.* SCh last at 3 ds.

Round 11: SR 4^4, <Ch 16, R 10+10 (to base of next R on previous round), Ch 5-6-6-6-6-6-5, R 10+10, Ch 16>. *R 4+4, <>.* SLJ and SCh at 16 ds.

Round 12: SR 11^11, <Ch 12 [Sh2: JR 10] 12, R 11+11 (to base of next main R on previous round), Ch 5, *R 4+4, Ch 3-3,* repeat * * 4 more times, R 4+4, Ch 5>. ***R 11+11, <>.*** SLJ.

Round 13: SR 11^11, <Ch 14-14, R 11+11 (to base of next R on previous round), Ch 6, *R 4+4, Ch 3-3,* repeat * * 3 more times, R 4+4, Ch 6>. ***R 11+11, <>.*** SLJ.

Round 14: SR 11^11, <Ch 10 [Sh2: JR 10] 10+ (to Ch p on previous round), Ch 10 [Sh2: JR 10] 10, R 11+11, Ch 12, *R 4+4, Ch 3-3,* repeat * * 2 more times, R 4+4, Ch 12>. ***R 11+11, <>.*** SLJ.

Round 15: SR 11^11, <Ch 16, R 7+7 (to JR on previous round)), Ch 16, R 7+7 (to next JR), Ch 16, R 11+11, Ch 16, *R 4+4, Ch 3-3,* repeat * * 1 more time, R 4+4, Ch 16>. ***R 11+11, <>.*** SLJ.

Round 16: SR 11^11, <Ch 12-12, R 11+11 (to base of next R on previous round), Ch 12-12, R 11+11, Ch 12-12, R 11+11, Ch 18, R 4+4, Ch 3-3, R 4+4, Ch 18>. *R 11+11, <>.* SLJ.

Round 17: SR 11^11, <Ch 14, R 11+11 (to Ch p on previous round), Ch 14, R 11+11, Ch 18, R 11+11 (to Ch p), Ch 18, R 11+11, Ch 14, R 11+11 (to Ch p), Ch 14, R 11+11, Ch 8 [Sh2: JR 10] 8, R 4+4, Ch 8 [Sh2: JR 10] 8>. *R 11+11, <>.* SLJ.

Dahlia Doily 1

MATERIALS

2 tatting shuttles

DMC Cordonnet, size 30

SIZE

6 inches

INSTRUCTIONS

Round 1: R 7-3—3-7, Ch 4 [Sh2: JR 10] 3, Sh2: R 5—5-5—5, Ch 4 [Sh2: JR 10] 3. *R 7+3—3-7, Ch 4 [Sh2: JR 10] 3, Sh 2: R 5—5-5—5, Ch 4 [Sh2: JR 10] 3.* Repeat * * 7 more times. Total 9 Rs and Chs. SLJ.

Note: Refer to the photo for the direction of the chains.

Round 2: *R 5—5+ (to any middle R p on previous round) 5—5, Ch 4-4-4-4-4-4-4.* SCh at last 4 ds.

Round 3: SR 3^3, <Ch 6, *R 3+3 (to next Ch p on previous round), Ch 3-3,* repeat * * 4 more times>. ***R 3+3, <>.*** SCh at last 3 ds.

Round 4: SR 4^4, <Ch 10, *R 4+4 (to next Ch p on previous round), Ch 3-3,* repeat * * 3 more times>. ***R 4+4, <>.*** SCh at last 3 ds.

Round 5: SR 5^5, <Ch 20, *R 5+5 (to next Ch p on previous round), Ch 4-4,* repeat * * 2 more times>. ***R 5+5, <>.*** SCh at last 4 ds.

Round 6: SR 5^5, <Ch 16-16, *R 5+5 (to next Ch p on previous round), Ch 4-4,* repeat * * 1 more time>. ***R 5+5, <>.*** SCh at last 4 ds.

Round 7: SR 4^4, <Ch 12-12, R 4+4 (to next Ch p on previous round), Ch 12-12, R 4+4, Ch 4-4>. *R 4+4, <>.* SCh at last 4 ds.

Round 8: SR 3^3, <Ch 20, R 3+3 (to next Ch p on previous round), Ch 28, R 3+3, Ch 20>. *R 3+3, <>.* SLJ.

Dahlia Doily 2

MATERIALS
2 tatting shuttles

DMC Cordonnet, size 30

SIZE
7 inches

INSTRUCTIONS

Round 1: R 7-3—3-7, Ch 4 [Sh2: JR 10] 3, Sh2: R 5—5-5—5, Ch 4 [Sh2: JR 10] 3. *R 7+3—3-7, Ch 4 [Sh2: JR 10] 3, Sh 2: R 5—5-5—5, Ch 4 [Sh2: JR 10] 3.* Repeat * * 7 more times. Total 9 Rs and Chs. SLJ.

Note: Refer to the photo for the direction of the chains.

Round 2: *R 5—5+ (to any middle R p on previous round) 5—5, Ch 4-4-4-4-4-4-4.* SCh at last 4 ds.

Round 3: SR 3^3, <Ch 6, *R 3+3 (to next Ch p on previous round), Ch 3-3,* repeat * * 4 more times>. ***R 3+3, <>.*** SCh at last 3 ds.

Round 4: SR 4^4, <Ch 10, *R 4+4 (to next Ch p on previous round), Ch 3-3,* repeat * * 3 more times>. ***R 4+4, <>.*** SCh at last 3 ds.

Round 5: SR 5^5, <Ch 4-4-4-4-4, *R 5+5 (to next Ch p on previous round), Ch 4-4,* repeat * * 2 more times>. ***R 5+5, <>.*** SCh at last 4 ds.

Round 6: SR 5^5, <Ch 8, *R 3+3 (to next Ch p on previous round), Ch 3-3,* repeat * * 2 more times, R 3+3, Ch 8, *R 5+5, Ch 4-4,* repeat * * 1 more time>. ***R 5+5, <>.*** SCh at last 4 ds.

Round 7: SR 4^4, <Ch 16, *R 4+4 (to next Ch p on previous round), Ch 3-3,* repeat * * 1 more time, R 4+4, Ch 16, R 4+4, Ch 4-4>. ***R 4+4, <>.*** SCh at last 4 ds.

Round 8: SR 3^3, <Ch 14-14, R 5+5 (to next Ch p on previous round), Ch 4-4, R 5+5, Ch 14-14>. *R 3+3, <>.* SCh at last 14 ds.

Round 9: SR 4^4, <Ch 30, *R 4+4 (to next Ch p on previous round), Ch 22,* repeat * * 1 more time>. ***R 4+4, <>.*** SLJ.

Dahlia Doily 3

MATERIALS

2 tatting shuttles

DMC Cordonnet, size 30

SIZE

13.5 inches

INSTRUCTIONS

Round 1: R 7-3—3-7, Ch 4 [Sh2: JR 10] 3, Sh2: R 5—5-5—5, Ch 4 [Sh2: JR 10] 3. *R 7+3—3-7, Ch 4 [Sh2: JR 10] 3, Sh 2: R 5—5-5—5, Ch 4 [Sh2: JR 10] 3.* Repeat * * 7 more times. Total 9 Rs and Chs. SLJ.

Note: Refer to the photo for the direction of the chains.

Round 2: *R 5—5+ (to any middle R p on previous round) 5—5, Ch 4-4-4-4-4-4.* SCh at last 4 ds.

Round 3: SR 3ˆ3, <Ch 6, *R 3+3 (to next Ch p on previous round), Ch 3-3,* repeat * * 4 more times>. ***R 3+3, <>.*** SCh at last 3 ds.

Round 4: SR 4ˆ4, <Ch 10, *R 4+4 (to next Ch p on previous round), Ch 3-3,* repeat * * 3 more times>. ***R 4+4, <>.*** SCh at last 3 ds.

Round 5: SR 5ˆ5, <Ch 20, *R 5+5 (to next Ch p on previous round), Ch 4-4,* repeat * * 2 more times>. ***R 5+5, <>.*** SCh at last 4 ds.

Round 6: SR 5ˆ5, <Ch 16-16, *R 5+5 (to next Ch p on previous round), Ch 4-4,* repeat * * 1 more time>. ***R 5+5, <>.*** SCh at last 4 ds.

Round 7: SR 4ˆ4, <Ch 12-12, R 4+4 (to next Ch p on previous round), Ch 12-12, R 4+4, Ch 4-4>. *R 4+4, <>.* SCh at last 4 ds.

Round 8: SR 3ˆ3, <Ch 10-10, R 3+3 (to next Ch p on previous round), Ch 28, R 3+3, Ch 10-10>. *R 3+3, <>.* SCh at last 10 ds.

Round 9: SR 5—5ˆ5—5, <Ch 4-4-4-4-4, R 5—5ˆ5—5 (to next Ch p on previous round), Ch 4-4-4-4-

4-4-4-4-4-4-4-4-4-4>. *R 5—5+5—5, <>.* SCh at last 4 ds.

Round 10: SR 3ˆ3, <Ch 6, *R 3+3 (to next Ch p on previous round), Ch 3-3,* repeat * * 2 more times, R 3+3, Ch 6, *R 3+3, Ch 3-3,* repeat * * 11 more times>. ***R 3+3, <>.*** SCh at last 3 ds.

Round 11: SR 3ˆ3, <Ch 6, *R 3+3 (to next Ch p on previous round), Ch 3-3,* repeat * * 1 more time, R 3+3, Ch 6, *R 3+3, Ch 3-3,* repeat * * 10 more times>. ***R 3+3, <>.*** SCh at last 3 ds.

Round 12: SR 3ˆ3, <Ch 10, R 3+3 (to next Ch p on previous round), Ch 3-3, R 3+3, Ch 10, *R 3+3, Ch 3-3,* repeat * * 9 more times>. ***R 3+3, <>.*** SCh at last 3 ds.

Round 13: SR 4ˆ4, <Ch 18, R 4+4 (to next Ch p on previous round), Ch 18, *R 4+4, Ch 4-4,* repeat * * 8 more times>. ***R 4+4, <>.*** SCh at last 4 ds.

Round 14: SR 4ˆ4, <Ch 4-4-4-4-4-4-4-4, *R 4+4 (to next Ch p on previous round), Ch 4-4,* repeat * * 7 more times>. ***R 4+4, <>.*** SCh at last 4 ds.

Round 15: SR 4ˆ4, <Ch 6, *R 4+4 (to next Ch p on previous round), Ch 3-3,* repeat * * 5 more times, R 4+4, Ch 6, *R 4+4, Ch 4-4,* repeat * * 6 more times>. ***R 4+4, <>.*** SCh at last 4 ds.

Round 16: SR 5ˆ5, <Ch 10, *R 5+5 (to next Ch p on previous round), Ch 3-3,* repeat * * 4 more times, R 5+5, Ch 10, *R 5+5, Ch 4-4,* repeat * * 5 more times>. ***R 5+5, <>.*** SCh at last 4 ds.

Round 17: SR 4ˆ4, <Ch 18, *R 4+4 (to next Ch p on previous round), Ch 3-3,* repeat * * 3 more times, R 4+4, Ch 18, *R 4+4, Ch 4-4,* repeat * * 4 more times>. ***R 4+4, <>.*** SCh at last 4 ds.

Round 18: SR 4ˆ4, <Ch 5-5-5-5-5, *R 4+4 (to next Ch p on previous round), Ch 4-4,* repeat * * 2 more times, R 4+4, Ch 5-5-5-5-5, *R 4+4, Ch 4-4,* repeat * * 3 more times>. ***R 4+4, <>.*** SCh at last 4 ds.

Round 19: SR 4ˆ4, <Ch 6, *R 4+4 (to next Ch p on previous round), Ch 3-3,* repeat * * 2 more times, R 4+4, Ch 6, *R 4+4, Ch 5-5,* repeat * * 1 more time, R 4+4, Ch 6, *R 4+4, Ch 4-4,* repeat * * 2 more times, R 4+4, Ch 6, *R 4+4, Ch 5-5,* repeat * * 2 more times>. ***R 4+4, <>.*** SCh at last 5 ds.

Round 20: SR 3ˆ3, <Ch 16, *R 3+3 (to next Ch p on previous round), Ch 4-4,* repeat * * 1 more time, R 3+3, Ch 16, R 3+3, Ch 5-5, R 3+3, Ch 16, *R 3+3, Ch 4-4,* repeat * * 1 more time, R 3+3, Ch 16, *R 3+3, Ch 5-5,* repeat * * 1 more time>. ***R 3+3, <>.*** SCh at last 5 ds.

Round 21: SR 3ˆ3, <Ch 14-14, R 3+3 (to next Ch p on previous round), Ch 4-4, R 3+3, Ch 14-14, R 3+3, Ch 14-14, R 3+3, Ch 4-4, R 3+3, Ch 14-14, R 3+3, Ch 5-5>. *R 3+3, <>.* SCh at last 5 ds.

Round 22: SR 3ˆ3, <Ch 20, R 3+3 (to next Ch p on previous round), Ch 20, R 3+3, Ch 20, R 3+3, Ch

30, R 3+3, Ch 20, R 3+3, Ch 20, R 3+3, Ch 20>. *R 3+3, <>.* SLJ.

Biography

Hye-oon Lee was born in South Korea and moved to the United States at the age of twenty-four. She started tatting while raising her two daughters as a stay-at-home mom. Within a year of learning how to tat, she started designing her own patterns. Most of her design inspiration comes from nature, and she is particularly fond of flowers. Her other interests include gardening, hiking, and traveling. She currently resides with her family in Seattle, Washington.

Made in the USA
Monee, IL
10 September 2020